Heart Journey

Altina Truss

BookLeaf Publishing

India | USA | UK

Presentation by *BookLeaf Publishing*

Web: www.bookleafpub.com

E-mail: info@bookleafpub.com

ISBN: 9789360943875

First edition 2024

*To every person that has had a broken heart
or had to heal from past pains...walk
through My Heart Journey. I hope you find
something you can relate to or hold on to.*

ACKNOWLEDGEMENT

All The People That Caused My Hurts & Pains, God, The Universe, The Ancestors, The Aliens & Mother Earth. Thank you all ... I wouldn't have made it here without you.

PREFACE

Healing is an individual journey that every person should make... Know that you are never alone on the journey... Even when it seems lonely... Better Days Are Coming!!!

Rollercoaster Ride

Weee... We're up up up today
The sun is shining; no clouds in the sky
Up so high on a rollercoaster ride
Head thrown back; lots of laughter in the air
Oh...sharp turn; I felt as if I might be thrown
Hold On...another jerk...what the heck is going
on
Click Click Click; We are moving again
I can feel the sun on my skin
Down in a flash without the blink of an eye
My stomach is in my throat; I'm trying hard not
to lose my lunch
Oh my...a loop; I hope my safety harness isn't
loose
Final stretch; I can see the end..
One More Swoop and a few more clicks &
I have survived this rollercoaster ride my friend.

Super Power

When things get rough giving up is not an
   option..

Everybody falls short;
   try and try again; get focused...

Answers are not always the ones we want

Keep the course & play the cards you're dealt

No way is the only way; Keep that in Mind

Every Action has a Reaction

Sometimes it's up to us to decide

See it for weakness or growth...

When I am weak then I am made strong...

2 Corinthians 12:9

My grace is sufficient for thee: for my strength
is made perfect in weakness

Cut Ties

Let go of hate
So all haters must go
They will be dealt with later
Not letting anyone stop your flow
Keep success on your mind
Now's time to grind
Anyone or anything not on that can go
Let no one and nothing bring you down
Don't let negatives hang around
Keep it going
Now it's time to cut ties
Let nothing and no one steal your shine
You have to let go
Cut Ties

Why Should I Care

Why should I care when no one else does
Why should I shed all the tears...
Man & Woman equals no one or nothing in the
world today
Can I change that if only I care
Make me understand the cruelness of my people
Lord I bend my knees in prayer
Give me an answer... why should I care?
No one knows what's real anymore
No one else seems to care...
Why should I give to the needy?
I too am in need my dear
Can little ol' me change things?
Maybe so, maybe no...
I sit and I wait on my knees
Here I will stay until that one day
The good Lord answers me
Still the same question God...
Why should I care.....

New Beginnings

Unfulfilled Desires...
Fill my cup
Balance and Consistency...
Fill my cup
Prosperity & Financial Freedom...
Fill my cup
Higher Self...Let's Level Up
I will be patient with me
Do what it takes to keep me grounded today
Forgive often & accept the lesson
I'm learning to listen to my intuition
Now I know I must 1st fill my own cup
New Love; Learning to love myself

New Beginnings; Means I am no longer
Stressing
Victory Today Is Mine

Laugh To Keep From Crying

I laugh to keep from crying
Sometimes I kinda feel like I'm dying
The pain is so real it rocks my core
I can't hide it anymore...
Yet, I'm trying....
I laugh to keep from crying
It hurts so bad; why am I not dying
With pain this intense
Somebody would be kind to slit my wrist
No such luck...I sit here stuck
In torture and torment...

Left to handle this with my mind
I dive deep down inside
I search for the silver lining in my clouds
This chaos called my life...
No Matter the situation....Death, Dishonor,
Disdain & Dismay
I find a way to laugh at it all so the tears can
escape my face
I laugh to keep from crying & that is just my
way....

I'd rather make a bad joke than to let others
know I'm lying

So... I laugh...
I was told to use my mind
Turn it around and see it as if it's behind
No better way than a good chuckle
Take your mind off of your troubles
When you feel the tears fill your eyes
Go inside your own bubble...
Find the humor in the mess of things
Maybe even a temporary solution...
Simple as it seems...
I laugh to keep from crying

The Perfect Storm

No this is not normal..
One day it's Hot & Heavy
The next it's Cold As Ice
Seems that we just can't keep the temperature
steady to save a life
We twist and turn to no end
Neither of us is willing to give in
On a path of destruction picking up things along
the way
Now it's hard to see through the dabre what's
really going on in between
We start out going east and take a turn that takes
us south
We changed directions and now someone lost a
house
The sun was out…

There was silence…
Now there is a battle already happening
I didn't want this.. it happened too fast
The perfect storm…
Who knows how long it will last

In A Daze

So many ways I can say the same thing
Hello.. Hey…Howdy…How are you today?
Good bye…I'm leaving… Arrivederci!
I have practiced this my whole life building my
vocabulary..
I can be proper, I can be hood, I can switch up
based on the company I keep…
One thing I can't be is fake..
I don't understand…I won't ever try
I love me for who I am so nigga open your eyes
Don't need a fake accent or a haze of lies
Keep ya fake-ish…
I run this so there is no surprise
So when you left in the dust in a daze you know
why
I will keep improving my life
Leave a little bit of my essence

My genuine impression
Just know I'm gone... however I say Bye!!!

13

Day Break

The sky is dark and there is a chill in the air
No one is around and the streets are clear
To my right the city skyline twinkles
To my left a mountain view
I hold my head back and reminisce about old
times with you...
Why oh why did it have to end
Seems like I lost my best friend
I see a star in the sky as clear as day
I wish & I wish ... it suddenly fades away
Looking left and right and straight up I stare
Wondering if you too saw the star there
Hoping we had one more moment to share
Just as the tears roll down my face the darkness
begins to luminate
The sun starts to rise and reminds me
It's a new day...My troubles are over ...
Thank God For Day Break...

12452 Long Rd

12452 Long Rd
5:52 am cars rush up the drive
2 cops cars and the ambulance not far behind
I hear the officers yell out...
"Ma'am...drop the gun".
I raise my head and yell back
"Ok...Ok ...I'm done"
I place the weapon on the porch and just as I
start to rise...
The officers rush to me and I'm thrown on the
ground from the side...
Paramedics go rushing by with the stretcher and
a bunch of their supplies...

I explain "he's in there but he surely already died"...
"The man inside the house has tormented my life...
I lived in his shadow and was treated horribly as his wife"...
Nobody seemed to care...They have heard it all and there was no surprise...
I yelled out "don't you dare" as I struggled moving side to side...
"God...please don't let him be revived"...
"Lord…Today was the day ... I couldn't take it anymore"...
"It would be the last time that man crossed the line"...

As they lift me off the ground with my arms cuffed behind...
I tell the detective... he needs to hear my side...
He replied in a heavy tone "Let's see if he survives"...
I'm placed in the police car and from there it was a silent ride ...
Once the car stopped the cop announced ..."yep lady we've arrived"...
It seemed like only moments passed...
They whisked me quickly inside...
Placed me in a little room, just a table and 2 chairs on either side...

The room was so small; Barley closet size...

I could feel eyes were on me
At the window I gave a glare & gaze...
Tears filled my eyes making streaks down in
lines all over my face...
As the tears start to dry...
I am in a Daze...Feeling a bit dismayed...
I lower my head; look down toward my feet; like
the answer would be there to seek for what to
say....
When the door opened up...
Sitting there; Stuck
The detective came in and had a seat...
Started with introducing himself...
He did exactly what he said he would do for
me...
He wanted to listen and I kindly obliged...
I told him the real story of me...

As frantic as I was it felt good to tell…
That story was told…
I'd been through hell…
All of it...not just the happy times….
What a story… I had to explain…
He tormented me from the start in subtle ways...
I told him all about the beatings...
Him calling me out of my name...
Choking me almost unconscious...

Pulling fistfuls of my hair some days...
I told him about the busted lips and him
threatening my life every day ...
Not sure if my family was safe if he was still
alive...

I told him to check my phone
All the evidence is inside...
I knew that if he killed me 1st it was the only
chance I would have to speak from the other
side...
Someone else entered the room...
They informed him.. they had all they needed
for now ...
The man just died...forensic specialists are
outside...
She will have to be checked from head to toe...
They will need to confirm it...
Hopefully she has told no lies...
I lowered my head with 1 thing left to be said...
"12452 Long Rd"... "I'm glad to know he's
dead"
12 years 4 Love 5 year 2 Long is the road that I
was on"

IDGAF

Today is not the day...
I'll get it done my way...
Your opinion is unsolicited so go ahead and
walk away...
Tomorrow is not promised
Who cares what you have to say...
Talk about your own issues leave mine where it
lay ...
I guess you missed the message
I will say it like this if I may...
I Don't Give A Fuck
I was born to Slay…

Love or Loyalty

You can choose to love me
Some days it feels like hate
Correct me when I'm wrong
That love shit can go out the window some days
You can choose to respect me
I won't have it if you can't
No nigga, you can't sit here and play in my face
You can choose to live in honor
Do things the right way
If not you'll find yourself alone cause I won't
stick around or stay
I want love and respect but that honor goes a
million miles around all time and space
Either you are loyal or you are not
I don't do the fake smiles or play games...
Some choose love over loyalty time after time
But me I require loyalty like royalty

Baby I am a Queen & I'm calling court today
With that comes the love, the respect and honor
for when we go through the hard days
My ruling will favor loyalty in each and every
case
While others chose love
I will get that anyway

No Regrets

What's done is done
Yet I have had to overcome
Many demons I have had to slay...

My prayer life is stronger
Now that I have lived longer
I am thankful for every day...

I speak life into others
I drank of living water
I will overflow your cup darlin...

No concern for what to eat
What to wear?
I'm not bothered...

My father owns ..."Everything"
So do I!
Cause I am his daughter...

I hold my head high
Live with no regrets
No time for my crown to be fallin...

A brand new mantra daily

Beautiful, Confident & Abundant I Am baby
My energy is different, I choose to be this way..

My ancestors & the universe have guided me
The creator removed the scales from my eyes
Now I see things clearer everyday...

I have seen glimpses of
What the future holds
I sincerely have
No Regrets

Side Piece

I am not; I never will be
Qualified to be anyone's side piece...
I identify as a whole meal not a snack
So if that's what you thought
Run that shit back...

Not here to compliment what you already have
I'm the highlight; the superstar at dinner
Put ya chick next to me
You'll "f" around and set me free
You'll end up with nothing to eat cause I'm gone

I come complete with my head on
Bountiful Breast for you to rest on
Arms to wrap you up for comfort...

I can support you; I'll have ya back
When the time comes; I'm worth it
I have a purpose and I add something
She will never compare to me...

I will hold you tight when you need lovin
I am stuffed with abundance...
Between my thighs I hold a wish
Bone & we can bring forth new life...

This is my Public Service Announcement...
I Am Not Nor Will I Ever Be
Compared to anyone or anything...
If you are looking to have this meal
no side dishes required still...
I'm Everything you need to get your fill....
I Don't need a Label
I'm Never A Side Piece

Changing

I'm changing
You can call me changeling
You don't have to call me at all...

My energy
Trumps most frequencies
I have connected to the Devine...

Old Wounds
Are in new tombs
All that shit is dead and gone; I'm fine...

Clothes fresh
Hair & Nails on deck
My swag is swagging on y'all...

I'm manifesting
Damn near everything
Walking into my purpose on time...

So free
Now that my soul is clean
Healing from the inside feels sublime...

New days
Elevation to Big Stages
I've changed for the better in my mind...

Chakra Aligned

I have everything I want; I have everything I
need
I am happy; I feel wealthy
I do good to my fellow man

I love unconditionally; I speak positivity
I see my dreams materialized
Not just in my head

I know I am deserving of an extraordinary life
All the wonderful things the universe has for me

I am open; I'm hyper-focused
I am grateful for all I've achieved
Today I am the best version of myself

I have the power to transmute energy
My Chakra's Aligned; God is on time
To gain clarity sometimes you must separate
yourself

Family Stuff

No family is perfect certainly not mine
I love them each and every day
In and out of time...

My mother's love has always kept the whole
thing afloat
Not sure how she does it but she manages us so
well...

My father had a different way
Lord don't I miss his laugh these days....
He made everything a joke
Until you made him mad...

My oldest sister knows everything
Who better to trust than the professor of the
clan...

She can find fault in every word so be careful to
tell her just enough...

My middle sister has her own way
Truly the wild card everyday....
Her tribe can drive a sane man mad
Fussing and cussing all the time...

Me... I have the unique spot
Last one of the litter... where shit stops
Now that I'm bigger I have my own mind
I do what I want and some people get triggered
My kid is grown so I did my job

We may be different in every way
Our love remains the same...
We are a family no matter who's missing
We'll cut you bout messing with our name...

Our offspring are crazy
Some of us are dangerous
Please don't come for the kids...
We will make you regret it
Show up together
burn downtown like the devil...then leave

We all go back to our corners and chill on
purpose
Don't need too much time in the same place

We have a blast when we come together
When done we can walk away
Our business is finished
Save the rest of the family stuff for another day...

Love Wins

Life gets hard and the sun doesn't always shine
No matter what happens
Love won't just go away...

Clouds will come and go and sometimes it even
rains
God has given us a promise
Rainbows remind us these days...

In every situation there will be dark days
Don't doubt that the pain gets real
When you can't take much more
Remember that Love Wins Always…

My Oh My

My journey has just begun
Just as soon it will end
Seems to be done in the blink of an eye
I'm healing from the inside out

It feels good to be whole
Never stay down too long
God made sure I was built that way

The Dream

Thoughts of you creep into my mind all the time
Oh how sweet you do play in my head…

Your natural beauty and your care for me
Make me want you to stay In my bed…

I am under submission
Subdued by your mention
The realism is inviting that way; no dread…

I'm caught up in feelings with physical dealings
Our bodies fit perfect tangled together on
purpose
It somehow works.…

No matter who knows it
This was done by choice

It's kinda worth it…

Tomorrow's not promised
I enjoy all the moments
No one ever has to understand…

We're perfect together
No one does me better
Now my dream can come to an end…

Enough

I love you so much
I'm not giving up
On the journey I will find my way...

I will fuss, fight and argue
For you my daring
It's worth it if I have the final say...

No more hoping and wishing
True love I am giving
I'm done at the end of the day...

I need a break from this mission
Be back when you finished
Boy bye!!
I've had enough...